# BREATHING UNDERWATER

## A COLLECTION OF POEMS AND SHORT STORIES

## NICK HORGAN

**TSL Publications**

First published in Great Britain in 2017
By TSL Publications, Rickmansworth

Copyright © 2017 Nick Horgan
Cover by Nick Horgan

ISBN / 978-1-911070-87-0

# Contents

4

# Introduction

Thank you for picking up this book and opening it, but before you read this introduction please do go and read the poems and stories, and see what you think of them. If you like something let it sink in, and when you have I hope you find something real in there. And if you find you've got your own understanding and you don't want to read the introduction that's fair enough. So please skip over this for now ...

... welcome back, I hope you enjoyed the poems and short stories. So here's a bit about me:

The two questions I'm always asked about my writing are "what do you write about?" And "where do you get your ideas from?"

There's no straightforward answer. Occasionally I'm writing to fulfil a brief – a competition has rules, a calendar has a subject and a size restraint, an exhibition has a theme. More often I'm inspired by a song, a painting, a scene or a situation in a film, a phrase heard on the television, another poem, anything that's open to expansion, to examination, to applying to here and now, or taking in another direction. The result may be directly or obliquely related to the source. For example *Howl2012* takes a similar form as the original poem, whereas *Louder Than the Wind* has many more subtle influences and inspirations.

And often an idea is generated through a writing exercise, particularly those set at our writing group. Someone else setting a limited range of options forces me to examine topics I might never have considered. By the subject being taken out of my hands (to an extent) the challenge is to respond with something new. Some rock bands by the third album in have run out of new things to say because they only have a few issues to address (summarised somewhere as – I love you, I hate you, Come back, Go away, and Let's all get along). Being challenged to come up with something unexpected might produce a germ of an idea, but once it's there I may be able to coax some life into it. As long as I don't end up somewhere I've been before.

There's everything that's happening in the world, macro and micro, there's people and places, good experiences and bad experiences, memories, things unsaid, contradictions between what we see and what we know, connections between the physical and material and the emotional, spiritual, the constant change and comparison of modern life, and everything your imagination can open up, make connections, build up, revise, refocus, examine and explore to take you from the initial seed to a finished piece.

In our modern lives it's not easy to find the time to sit down and write, so the writing group provides that opportunity. And if inspiration strikes I'll have an idea to work on at home which is easier than starting from scratch.

Some ideas come almost full-formed, others take a while to reveal their possibilities, sometimes an idea is too slim and needs to be built up into something more substantial, and sometimes simple is best.

A few ideas, but not many, come from daydreaming in an armchair. More likely is that the answer to a question rather than the question itself comes to mind in the armchair, when the subconscious gets a chance to speak up. I might be day-dreaming about a holiday but as I sift through the memories something significant sticks out, or I notice a parallel with another subject, and there's a connection to explore.

If I hit on an idea that seems true to me, it will have a different significance for different readers. I can't tell how what I write will be taken, all I can do is choose the words that seem right, and rewrite, reconsider, and rewrite until the thing looks like it can stand on its own feet, look me and the reader in the eye and say "try me, what do I look like, to you?"

Even this introduction has been written several times, and then again from scratch, incorporating whatever I learned from the earlier revisions. There may be art in the initial idea but it's the craft in the shaping that brings it to life.

I find it very difficult to sit down and write unless there's a good clear stretch in front of me (so I can procrastinate tidying my desk, filing receipts and making lists of other things to do), and have no-one interrupting me. Maybe it's just me but I have to get so absorbed to trust what I'm doing that the idea of being interrupted, and having to reabsorb it all to get to where I was, puts me off starting. I did notice how precious that sounds.

And underlying everything I write, because it's part of who I am, is my faith. Sometimes it's obvious (*How Will You Answer My Prayer this Time?*), sometimes it's the unseen foundation (*The Earth Turns*). My faith underpins my hope for the future and my understanding of my place in the world, because I am reconciled, forgiven and free. I hope every poem has as its foundation: that all life is a gift, to be enjoyed, in relationships, in nature, in creativity and imagination, in communion with our maker; that life is harder for some and we cannot ignore that; that life as we know it does end, and we don't know quite what happens next, but we will be held to account for the choices we made; and that mankind has a saviour, no matter what. And I acknowledge that whatever measure of talent I have has been given as a free gift. It's a blessing not a halo. I hope it illuminates and resonates. It won't achieve that for everyone nor by the same degree. We all bring our own experiences to evaluate what we read and I can only write what I know or can imagine.

For this reason I disagree with competitions where a book or story is crowned the winner. I'm happy for work to be judged against a standard (shortlisting) but beyond that how can one story be "better" than another, except filtered through the experience and expectations of whoever judges. Which is better, *To Kill A Mockingbird* or *Lord of the Rings*? It all depends who you ask, by popular consensus they both exceed a standard and that's enough. I've been shortlisted three times and I genuinely accepted that as fulfilling my ambition at the time [no-one's going to believe that, but I've said it now].

Another question is, "How long have you been writing?" – well we are all writing every day, even if we're just telling an anecdote, reviewing a film or a song, or making a joke. Any time we have a choice over how much to tell and which words to use. I work in administration, and while there are obvious constraints, there are creative choices to make all the time about how I present information. But to answer the question as it was meant, I didn't like writing at school and I'm not prolific now. Some writers had written their first novel by age twelve, not me, I was too busy reading. I remember *Asterix* and *TinTin* borrowed from the library, and later the *Hardy Boys* and *Robin Hood*, and *King Arthur*, and books of cowboys, and teenage footballing sensations, and *Biggles* the fighter pilot and Ursula Le Guin's *Earthsea* Trilogy (which I will return to again and again). And that desire to get lost in a book hasn't left me, I just might now be reading more mature books.

For my O-level English Language exam I picked the argue-for-and-against option rather than write a story. My English teacher threatened to withdraw me from the English Literature exam. This wasn't based on my ability but because he was always catching me talking in class. Everyone talked in his class, but I was right behind four boys whose sport was to keep him occupied with a stream of questions for as long into the lesson as possible. So he was always looking in my direction. That's my story and I'm sticking to it. So studying English Lit at any higher level wasn't ever contemplated. I carried on reading and occasionally put something in writing, nothing significant.

I finished university with an economics degree which wasn't much use in the early 90s and a couple of years later I was invited to join the church magazine committee, which was a great experience. My first assignment was to write about my recent trip to the Far East with my brother. I interviewed several members of the congregation with interesting histories and I worked with some wise heads and met some wonderful old people who had stories I'd never have imagined of them. The committee was always looking for ideas for articles, anyone who'd been somewhere interesting, or had been on a group outing, and that lasted until the magazine was discontinued several years later.

And then really not much until in 2010 I answered an invitation in the local paper to a new writing group starting later in the year. Thanks to that invitation and now more than six years later I have enough material to put this collection together.

Poems are open to every reader's interpretation and I don't wish to short-cut your experience with a meaning or explanation to look out for. But context can be useful so I have given below a little background on some of the pieces:

**Louder Than the Wind** was written a long time ago on the back of an envelope, long before I joined a writing group and was inspired by a few John Mellencamp songs and *Like Water For Chocolate*. I hope this is the final version.

**Remember, Remember** – a bit of fun with the bonfire night story, honestly some of the rhymes are meant to be off-key.

**Howl2012-abridged** was inspired by the original *Howl* poem by Allen Ginsberg (1956) in its structure and subject matter, repetition and the adaptation of the first line, and the first line that breaks the repetition of "I saw" ("Those burning for the eternal"), although unlike his poem this does not reference individuals but swathes of humanity. There is further influence from the reactions and discussions following the summer riots in London of 2011, a general dissatisfaction with many aspects of modern life (greed – laziness – apathy), including my own.

It describes the worst aspects of modern life but clearly it's not the whole picture, there are many people doing many great things, but so much more could be done if everyone cared – considered – acted, either together or individually. Yes, it may sound judgemental, but where deserved. There is no reference to whether it is the fault of the parents, the schools, the police, the church, that wasn't the point, although the anaesthetising effects of material comfort are just under the surface, along with the price paid for that comfort elsewhere, a general ignorance/denial of our good fortune.

**She Runs to See the Falling Snow** – my wife had never seen snow fall before she came to England, and she is still as excited as a child every time. I love the snow too. The quietness, the noise when you walk in it, the clean blanket over everything.

**Unidentified and Unfinished** and **Into Thin Air** were both written for a local crime writing competition, my first ever "full-length" short stories, and both made the short list. *Unidentified and Unfinished* was written with Mark Strong in mind, so imagine him reading it if you like. Or if you know him, ask him to read it to you (and record it and send to me pleeease).

**The Salvaged Chair** was developed from a writing workshop. We were asked to start with an image of desire, and a wooden chair came to mind (from who knows where). Once I had that image and had confused the facilitator with it I was determined to make something of it.

I've heard there's a common reoccurring dream where you're in the supermarket and realise you've got no clothes on. Thankfully not one of mine, but quite a few people have laughed awkwardly. Do you have moments in life when you suddenly feel "everyone knows", or that you've been caught out? Or when you are on your own and you do something stupid and it feels like someone saw even though there's no one there? Or when you think something terrible and shameful, and you are sure everyone heard it out loud?

**The Waterwheel** was written and selected for the writing group's 2016 calendar.

**The Earth Turns** is inspired by the incredible photos we get from our astronauts looking back at our planet, so far from home.

**Breathing Underwater** – is a thank you to every writer who's ever captured my imagination.

**Duality** – this poem was inspired by a painting by Arne Davidson, and is for friends and family with dual nationality, or simply more than one place that's home.

**Father's Day –** no we don't, but it seems a bit mean now I've written a poem about it.

**Holiday With a Stranger** – the how-did-we-get-here and who-are-you moments that occur even now, looking back to being on holiday in South Africa before we were engaged.

**Nursery Rhyme for Modern Times** was written for an exhibition (Easter Joy & Justice) looking at the Easter Story and issues of social justice. The assigned scene was Pilate washing his hands of Jesus' fate, (even though he had all the authority, and the might of the Roman Empire behind him) and how that might relate to modern issues of justice. These are the notes provided for the exhibition:

Context – this is written as a nursery rhyme and could be sung as a skipping, hopping or clapping game, many traditional nursery rhymes may have originally had grim meanings, and this kids' rhyme refers to many terrible situations in the modern world.

– over time the context may be lost and lines could lose their specific meaning

– over time words or lines may change or be forgotten, and no doubt in the future kids will have new issues to deal with, and this will be part of the past.

Verse 4 – Nepali men have been recruited to build world cup stadia in Qatar where they live in appalling conditions, their passports held by employers, payments delayed, and many have died. The sponsors, FIFA, the Qataris, the contractors, have each passed on the responsibility. Meanwhile the fans don't know or don't care as long as there's football, and the brands deflect the bad publicity.

– Drones causing civilian casualties as Saudi Arabia bombs the Yemen. The Saudis can't take their western allies out for a drink, but can still get unruly, deploying their latest purchases.

**Surrendered Judgement** was also written for the Easter Joy & Justice exhibition. The image of Pilate washing his hands is ideal to reference many issues of complacency, complicity, abdication of responsibility and cover-ups since his time.

**The Photographer's Assistant** – the first scene came out of a writing exercise and it's expanded from there. The "old-fashioned morality" was influenced by the moral code of the central character in *Parade's End* (book and television series).

**Into the Everlasting** – an other-world transportation story as an analogy, inspired and influenced by CS Lewis.

***

Thank you to Sundeep Kaur for initiating the Pinner Writers Group, to Barbara Towell for her leadership and commitment, and to all the members past and present for their support and encouragement, and their critical ear too, without which this wouldn't be worth publishing.

Thanks to Anne Samson at TSL Publications.

And finally thanks to my wife Berenice for forgiving me every time I forgot home-time or bed-time because "I just needed to get it written down before I lost it, and then I was on a roll, and I didn't realise how late it was."

*Nick Horgan*
*2017*
www.nickhorgan.com

# Louder Than the Wind

The band played downwind,
notes reached out struggling to be heard, before blowing back
  down and away,
and the wind, leaning everything across the scene, rushing
  across my senses
around my head, tugging my coat.

Now we can see the band,
puppet strings pull the dancers around the fires,
faster and higher, coats and skirts rising with the spin of fair-
  ground rides,
separating layers and twisting and weaving through each other,
the music fighting harder,
playing a rollercoaster ride through the air,
drawn and pulled nearer, we spin through the colours, faces,
  and the floating wings,
coats, that before settling over me, twist away beyond me and
  back,
dresses brush past, grounded hot air balloons,
catching and pulling past the faces, turning orange and black,
as the firelight glazes each shiny surface with pools of light,
dancing flames lick each face and figure with amber, now the
  sun has bedded down,
and the band played faster and looser, notes tumbling and
  dancing themselves.
later I woke in a pile of friends,
old friends and brand new old friends
she took her head off my collar,
loose hair slipping down her cheek
and whispered to me, louder than the wind,
something perfect in that moment.

## How Will You Answer My Prayer This Time?

How will you answer my prayer this time?
will you answer with rolling thunder, that crackles and bangs
will you answer like the dew in the grass
appearing from nowhere, now visible and physical,

How will you answer my prayer this time?
with an earthquake, with a meteorite
or, like the first flowers of spring
patient faith rewarded.

# In the Eye of the Ellipse

Looking out, there's a crease in the view,
a crumpled line where the blue and the green are crimped
  together,
disrupting each other's clarity,
where the concentration of my eye cannot prise them apart,

From that horizon, the ground swept back under my feet,
  the undertow fast and unbalancing,
and from the fold at the horizon the sky flew back over my
  head, too fast for my hands to catch,
the wash escaping through my fingers,

I turned and saw them racing away, the sky and the ground,
one bent up and one bent down, and somewhere ahead,
  at an unreachable distance,
they merged at the limit of my sight,
and I saw myself at the bottom of the frame, in the eye of their
  ellipse.

# The Sun Came Out Today

The sun came out today
Illuminating every leaf and blade
Insects buzzed through the floating dust
And bending petals stretched out in the welcome rays
And cast warm shadows through the light

The sun didn't show today
Heavy heads stared down at the ground
Huddled shut and swaying in the draft
Casting no shadows from the thin grey light to the frozen
  ground
Waiting and shivering for something to change
The sun didn't show today and neither did you

# Remember, Remember

Guy Fawkes is the name we always remember
he's the reason for bonfires on the 5th of November

In the heart of London under Westminster Palace
Guy Fawkes was hidden with explosives and malice

His plan was to blow up the House of Lords
and then run away to France on a horse

He had 36 barrels of top-grade gunpowder
can you imagine any noise louder?

The explosion would have woken the nation
but, there was no deadly detonation

No one knows who sent the king the warning
but Guy Fawkes was arrested early that morning

He was still waiting for the right moment
to blow up the houses of parliament

He was caught red-handed
and the gang disbanded

Some fled to the midlands, hotly pursued
leaving this Guy, facing the noose

And they found him guilty with very good reason
so they hung him to die for treacherous treason

So enjoy your bangers and hot chocolate
and remember Guy Fawkes and the gunpowder plot

Foiled by a letter sent from "anonymous"
now with bonfire nights – synonymous

# HOWL2012 – Abridged

I saw the best minds of my generation destroyed by greed, laziness, apathy, rolling drunk in the streets while their brothers were ordered to invade sovereign states to secure the drug of developed nations, to proclaim democracy, equality and self-determination,

I saw the bodies of generations destroyed by warfare, suicide bombers, genocide, collateral damage, friendly fire, pre-emptive strikes, slaughtered by blind greed, fundamentalism, and pride, piled up body bags in anticipation of the avoidable loss, women and children not spared, condemned to participate by equality and coercion,

I saw stricken seabirds greased and feeble, the last of species expire, rising floods and withering crops, man's vicious footprint across his inheritance,

I saw the peaceful protests of those who identified the greed with the destruction, beaten by those sworn to protect and serve, protests hijacked by anarchy and destruction, and I saw tsunamis of the will overpowering oppression,

I saw the best lives of my generation strung out on credit, their investments gambled by the bonus boys, gambled over and over, double or nothing always ending in nothing, who blamed Wall Street and the euro-zone for their collapsed lifestyle when the cheque bounced back into their dirty hands, dirty with the sweat of poverty in foreign lands, where you could and you would refuse to work, in conditions you chose not to know, your excuse not to care,

I saw the souls of a generation die, a generation who tamed ideas reducing them to icons and tamed those icons reducing them to t-shirts or hanging from chains, the dead Argentinian-Cuban, the crucified Jew, flattened and silenced,

I saw a generation too talented for fame-shows but, weighed down by celebrity media gluttony, short-sightedness born of media-fed insecurities, could raise their aspirations no higher, a generation embracing social media, to bully and mock, spreading new diseases for a new century, through our latest toy,

A generation who are not appalled by people trafficking, extreme poverty, forced marriages, honour killings, hate crimes, civilian casualties, child abuse, child labour, child soldiers, state sanctioned torture, female circumcision mutilation, the mutilation of our DNA in the name of science, the abandonment of the weak in body and mind, the sucking dry of the natural world, and the vomit left behind,

For whom life is not enough, imagination an insufficient gift, where the body is poisoned and punished to achieve escape, who sneer with derision at the hopeful, the active, the committed, the caring,

I saw a generation confused, angry and guilty for the out working of evil stretching back centuries, still seeing slavery in the colour of skin, still unable to silence dead Nazis, still waiting for Dr King's dream, still acting out of fear of power and retribution, hatred and suspicion,

*Those burning for the eternal heavenly connection to beyond the pin-pricked blackness of the nocturnal sky awake from your isolated pockets of consideration, who still their knowledge and doubts in expectation of enlightenment, induced by imagination not hallucination, by exchanges not defensiveness, and wait, for epiphanies that break through noise, conformity and selfishness,*

*Stand for this generation, whose restlessness is manipulated and criminalised and punished, exploited, herded and glorified,*

Who inhale despite science, who copulate without connection, and drink despite beauty, and inject despite love, in spite of love. Who don't read despite wisdom, won't wait despite consequences and don't vote despite history,

Who die alone on foreign fields, in hospital beds, in drunken wrecks, where they fell, alone but for the angels who carried them home, while family and friends sobbed and crossed hearts and left flowers you couldn't smell, to the eternal dilemma,

Who let their minds sag to quicksand consuming mass entertainment pumped out with sugar coating, sweet and sour sauce, and high levels of fat and salt, copied and pasted from one era to the next,

Congratulate yourselves for children in need, comic relief, sport relief, red nose day, marathon sponsors and the secret policeman's ball and be ashamed of the empty year in-between,

Whose only aspiration is to be judged as cool, as cool as those whose worth was once measured in teenage screams, rebellious poses, offended parents – the song remains the same, only the technology changes,

Future generations – there's no clean water
Future generations – the conflict is endless
Future generations – here's what you could have won if there had been anything left

*Those still burning for the eternal heavenly connection,*
*to the dreamers, the leaders, the warriors,*
*the wise and the wilful, the icons and idols,*
*the pure in spirit who can outlast the pornography around them,*
*through courage, imagination and grace,*
*take hold of the apathy, and the feral debauchery,*
*and breathe life back into the souls of this generation,*

*Look into the eyes of the dispossessed and see we are the same,*
*and rage against the dying lights within,*

We're with you in drought,
We're with you in poverty and, disease,
We're with you in homelessness, in loneliness, in boredom and despair, living on rubbish heaps, in hostels, in overcrowded hospitals and overcrowded jails, with you in endless power-cuts, in the queue for democracy, in the queue for water, in the queue for handouts, in the slums of communism, and the mirages of materialism as you are repossessed,

We are with you at the graves of departed souls, as you live and love and pray.

# She Runs to See
# The Falling Snow

She runs to see the falling snow,
bouncing on her toes at the window she calls for the camera,
to catch the memory before it melts away,
– it's so beautiful – will it stay?
– look it's collecting on the window – does that mean it will last?

She's still as excited as the first time,
She calls her family just to tell them, half the world away,
  how beautiful it is,
and she will send the photos,
but they can't understand,
they've never had snow falling outside their windows,

Hat, gloves, scarf, boots,
scrunching each step, into the silent white,
Looking up into the soft feathers falling,
cold and wet on flushed cheeks,
Dissolving on tongues too quick to be tasted,
so excited she doesn't feel the cold today.

# Asthma

I breathe
listening to the rattle of a train that never arrives
listening to it strain uphill, never reaching the summit

the earth breathes quietly, imperceptibly
buried alive
I breathe the movement of a thousand years in one breath

the ground heaves upward and the earth splits
roots are uncovered, soil trickles, nothing breaks through
the straining ends then falls slowly
crumbling crevasses close and all is buried again

the tyrant sits on my chest laughing
a straitjacket holds me from striking out
my mouth is open but his hand is on my throat
my wooden lungs creak, dry and splintering

I long for flooding, filling, escape, release
I breathe hard and listen
the train whistles and grinds its gears
I breathe hard, and listen for the gasping to recede

# Unidentified and Unfinished

You know why it's so hard to pull off big crimes and get away cleanly? Because of all the other monkeys involved. There's a whole list of them, the inside guy, the getaway drivers, the fence, officers on the take, lookouts, false alibis, code-breakers – anyone of these can give you away. The best planned job only needs one undercover cop somewhere in the set-up, or one schmuck who gives himself away buying a Ferrari with cash, to bring the whole thing crashing onto your front lawn.

And if the police can't catch you there's insurance investigators and tax inspectors, sticking their beaks in, pokin' about, "following the money".

That's why I work alone.

It's risk management – with all the CCTV, and camera phones everywhere and the quality of forensics these days – I don't need the extra aggravation.

Sorry, we haven't been introduced, I'm Harry,

Harry who? – Harry whoever you like – I'm not telling you.

I'm very very careful. I'm not in it for the glory, and I don't need the camaraderie – like I said they're all monkeys, throwing their crap at each other, sticking their arses out in public, drawing attention to being where they don't belong.

For me it's the satisfaction of executing the job, clean and efficient like a bullet train, but untraceable like a fingerprint in a puddle.

I don't leave clues and I avoid leaving patterns, so nothing leads back to me.

My only weak link is dead, and what do dead men tell? Exactly.

It wasn't my doing, but it was a rather convenient coincidence. This high-flying investment banker sets me up an offshore account. A month later he's low-lying, in his grave. The Russian mafia were implicated, which thankfully ruled me out.

And that account, despite only starting at a hundred grand, became my trump card, my passport to being above suspicion.

Conspicuous consumption? – yes, I have an offshore account – oh very good sir, we'll leave you and your millions in peace then.

Now I move in circles where everything is assumed and no questions are asked. I've become the living embodiment of the story I've told. Where was I on the night of the fifth? No-one's ever asked – because that would be outrageous.

I'm no Robin Hood, I keep what I take, but I only take from the criminal core. That's my style. They deserve nothing, except pain and loss, and nasty surprises.

I don't brag, I don't advertise, and I don't put my trust in other people.

I avoid alcohol, narcotics and the other pleasures that can cost you dear, remember – loose talk costs lives.

Now that I've been comfortably invisible for a while I might branch out, maybe bake artisan bread, join a jazz fusion orchestra, photograph endangered species, apply for space-camp, you know, widen my appeal – what do you think?

Professional suicide? Maybe – they say suicide can be a cry for help – but I'm probably just a tad bored.

If they ever arrest me it's because I stopped playing. I came out from my hiding place. They were never going to find me and I've called it off, game over. That's the only way they'll catch me.

But stealing from criminals requires especially careful plans, extra preparation and attention to detail, because if they catch you it's not five years at Her Majesty's Pleasure with all the privileges, the last year in an open prison, come and go as you like, thank you Ma'am. It's a bit more serious, torture and extortion for as long as you can take it, until you can't take it anymore.

How did it all start?

Well, it was a while ago, I'm not saying more than that – what were you expecting?

Dates and postcodes and photos?

Actually, I was starting my life again, and fate provided the trigger. My *St Valentine's Day Massacre* moment – have you seen *Some Like It Hot*? – you've not? – you should, daft yet charming. Except my witnessing of a crime was not witnessed itself.

*** 

I was taking a short cut to a station. It was late evening, not quite throwing out time. Ahead of me this chump was coming my way, but a hundred yards off he got jumped.

I fell back into the shadows unseen. They kicked him to the ground, and gave him a nasty vicious beating.

"Remember who did this to you," they were screaming, kicking his curled up body. Now, I can handle myself, could then, but this wasn't my fight and there were two of them.

As they circled him, bloody and tattered, I could clearly see their faces, and I knew who they were.

One had a knife. "Never forget this," he hissed as he crouched down, pressing it into his victim's face, testing the force needed to split the skin.

"Never forget, we run this town, this was your first and only warning."

"Payment, double, tomorrow," the other barked.

They picked up his briefcase, stamped open the lock and shook the contents out until the case hung empty like a happy dog's mouth.

"Tomorrow!" he barked again, and they were gone.

Inside me rose an anger I had never felt before. Not sympathy for this man broken before me, but a controlled rage, infecting every part of me, an indignation starting in my gut, and spreading as if I was being charged up.

That's how it started, from standby to full power, ready to go.

I turned and walked away, someone else would call an ambulance. For a day I raged within – that was not right – I couldn't express it more eloquently to myself than that. And as the day drew on a plan started to form, a plan that would again keep me in the shadows.

*** 

Theo and Morris Payne were spoilt thugs, sons of a self-made hard man, new money and no class, who'd graduated from terrorizing the playground as The Pain and More Pain, to running protection, money laundering, and safe houses for their father and his associates, with drug dealing on the side.

I could've burnt down their house, poisoned their dogs, and stolen their cars, but the insurance would replace it all. What was needed was the destruction of their influence. A dish served cold, and out of the blue.

I got myself into character, and called Theo, told him I was doing a deal with Morris, who was being a dick. I'd threatened to deal with Theo but Morris had laughed and said that prick wouldn't be able to handle it, (or words to that effect). I was offering the deal to Theo if he could beat Morris's price. And I'd make sure Payne senior heard all about it.

Like a red rag to a bull and, excuse me for mixing my metaphors, he took the bait.

Sibling rivalry eh? – one of life's great constants.

Who's your supplier he asked, I made something up about Columbians being raided and I'd been left holding the stash. He bought that – thick as thieves they say – and he certainly was.

I told him to meet me later in the Bridal shop on the High Street, we'd use the back office.

He wasn't to know the owner was away.

I got there early and broke in the back quietly. I unlocked the shop, drew the curtains across the front windows and waited.

Theo walked straight in through the front door, the muppet, which made it easy for me to jump him with the old chloroform-on-a-rag trick. He never even saw my masked face.

I dressed the scene and left out the back, casually.

Someone called the local paper and the local police to report the break in, from a payphone. Untraceable.

A crowd quickly gathered, tacking pictures with their phone, then the local press arrived, then the TV, and finally the cops.

Theo was sitting on a gold throne wearing a wedding dress 'fit for a princess', handcuffed into place, foaming at the mouth. The chloroform had worn off and Theo was wide-awake to his predicament.

The police, bless 'em, dragged him out screaming, dragged him out still in drag, still on his throne, past a wide-eyed Morris and Old Man Payne and dumped him on the kerb to prolong his humiliation.

Did I mention that whoever called the police had used Morris's name?

Soon Theo was accusing Morris of setting him up. Morris knew Theo had gone behind his back and screwed up. So they screamed abuse at each other while the film crews broadcast live to the nation.

The cross-dresser and the brother who grassed him.

The end of an era.

Peace in our time.

And Theo's £25k in my pocket.

All it took was a bit of forward thinking.

When you know your target's weaknesses, and the weaknesses of their hierarchy, and when you know the reactions of the police, the media, and the good old general public who are so predictable, you have all you need. A simple plan becomes a masterpiece, a symphony of moving pieces.

That is how I started.

# Into Thin Air

So here we are, a private airfield somewhere near the coast of East Anglia. The consignment has been checked for authenticity, the money transfer confirmed, weapons stood down, hands shaken and backs slapped, and ways departed. It had gone without a hitch, exactly as planned. Now for a cup of tea and the morning papers.

Back at the scene of the crime, the private TRA art gallery on the 8th floor of the exclusive Azure House, two detectives were struggling to piece together the events of the past few hours.

Detective Harris had arrived late, what with it being early Monday morning and no-one having died. Detective Jones, his junior partner, had already been there for some time, questioning security staff and having all CCTV footage reviewed.

"So, how did they get in and out?" Harris asked wearily.

"It's not clear Sir, there's no sign of entry except for one tiny window open in the men's room, there's no sign anyone was here, except for the paintings being missing. Internal surveillance was disabled for a few minutes and by the time security got up here they were gone."

Jones continued, "The window's too small to climb through, all the other floors are secure, and the fire escapes are intact."

"Could they have got in from the roof?"

"The roof Sir?"

"From a helicopter?"

"Too noisy."

"Or by parachute?"

"Too risky, it was pretty windy last night, and anyway the roof door was locked, I've got a dog team up there now, Sir."

"Very good, so if they didn't break in, were they already in?"

"What, hiding somewhere?"

"Yes detective, hiding or standing very still."

Detective Harris rubbed his still bloodshot eyes.

"And how the hell did they get out? How big's this window?"

"Only a child could squeeze through, and anyone climbing up or down outside would be seen on camera, they've been though all the footage and they're double checking it now, Sir. I also have an officer checking security footage at the surrounding buildings."

"So why was the window open?"

Harris's question was interrupted by the arrival of the Forensics Team who he waved away to the far end of the gallery where the walls were bare.

"Bloody CSI wannabees – the paintings will be half way to South America and they'll tell us what colour socks we're looking for!"

"Do we know exactly what's missing?"

"The whole collection Sir, due to be unveiled tomorrow, here's the brochure."

Harris read aloud, unimpressed, "For the first time ever, eight masterpieces brought together by the private TRA art gallery, which consider the philosophical and hypersurealistic blah blah arty schmarty waffle waffle blah. Basically eight paintings. What sizes are we talking about?"

"Security said the smallest was about thirty by twenty centimetres."

"What's that in old money?" asked Harris.

"Dunno Sir – a page of A4? The largest was a metre square – that's three foot by three foot Sir."

"Really? And they vanished into thin air, no way in no way out, one open window no one climbed through. Marvellous. We'd better have a look at those tapes."

The two detectives took the lift down to the third floor security room where the CCTV footage was held.

Harris asked to see footage showing the window.

"Well we've enhanced the picture as best we can, and you might just make out a shadow here," said Thomson, the officer in charge.

Harris and Jones squinted. A vague shape, barely visible in the morning gloom fell from the window and off the screen. "You wouldn't see it if you weren't looking."

Harris raised an eyebrow but let that one go.

His colleague spoke first, "If that bag contains the pictures rolled up, and this here," he pointed to a barely visible line, "is an anchored cord, they could slide the bag down the line, to the pavement, then reel the line in, job done."

"So who was waiting on the pavement, Thomson?"

"There were no pedestrians at that time, and any unregistered vehicles parked in the area would have been reported."

"Could they have driven past and picked up the bag rodeo-style? What footage do we have at street level?"

"We checked for escape vehicles earlier, there's nothing, a couple of empty taxis on the wrong side of the street, and the milkman."

"The milkman? Is he a regular? Was he on time? We'd better take a look, just in case."

Thomson enhanced and synchronized the pictures. They located a barrel-shaped bag lying on the pavement. Up pulled the milkfloat, partially obscuring the bag from both angles. The milkman got down, whistling. He casually delivered some milk and then looked up at one camera. He walked around his float, and while he was on the other side the bag disappeared. He jumped back on board and trundled off down the street and round the corner.

"And there it goes. So who are you Mr Gold Top?" mused Harris.

The tape was replayed.

"I think he winked at the camera," said Jones.

"The cheeky bugger," said Harris, "he did wink, zoom in a bit more, his face looked familiar. There he is, oh no he's wearing

33

a mask. It's Benny Hill, he's wearing a Benny Hill mask and he's winking at us, the cheeky bugger."

As the penny dropped Thomson said quietly, "Ernie, the fastest milkman in the west."

Harris released an obscenity. Jones was nonplussed.

"And he trundles out of sight and off-loads the paintings. Then I suppose he drives the milkfloat at full-speed into a wall, it explodes, destroying any evidence and showering everyone in great lumps of yoghurt."

"Sir?"

"You're too young," Thomson answered, "Google it when you get home, and any missing milkfloats."

A phone rang and Jones answered, it was the dog team on the roof, they'd found nothing, no scent, no equipment, no fresh abrasions on the perimeter, no sign of entry.

Another phone rang, Harris answered.

"Nothing? Okay, and you had clear sight of the roof all night, no choppers, hang-gliders, parachutists, abseillers, suicidal jumpers, high wire walkers? No, well thanks for checking."

"He's at the tower opposite," said Harris replacing the receiver, "they're three storeys higher with 24 hour surveillance and a clear view of our roof, and they've seen nothing. Our guys didn't come or go from the roof – we know how they got the art out, but did they get themselves out?"

"I'll get the Dog Unit to sweep the building, in case they're still here, Sir," Jones offered.

"Yes do, but if they've gone?"

"Thomson, before we arrived did you let anyone out downstairs, anyone who wasn't part of your team, anyone you didn't personally know?"

"No Sir, as soon as the theft was detected we initiated our emergency procedure, the front door and the delivery bay are the only ways in or out."

"And since we arrived and you've been up here?"

Thomson called the front door.

"They didn't let anyone out, except a couple of couriers who'd come in through deliveries to pick up a parcel. The front desk dealt with them, and then escorted them out through the front."

"Let me speak to them," said Harris, a fearful look crossing his face. He leaned over and turned on the speakerphone, "Tell us about these couriers you let out."

"We let them out because deliveries had let them in, how else would they have got in? Obviously we opened the package, we're not stupid, but it wasn't the paintings, just some paperwork from the gallery."

"And the delivery bay called you to say they were coming through?"

"Err no, the couriers said they'd been shown through, how else could they have got there, they didn't come through the front, we can see the door from here."

Thomson called the delivery bay, one delivery had been taken but no-one had been shown into the building. Harris let out another obscenity. Fearing the worst, the three men took the lift to the ground floor.

Harris marched to the reception desk, "Who signed for the package? What did they look like? Would you recognise them if you saw them again, and what's your name?" he demanded.

Anthony Donnelly introduced himself and handed over the courier schedule.

"I didn't get a good look, I was more concerned with the parcel, I was hoping it would be the paintings and when it wasn't I didn't pay them much more attention. One was short, with hair, the other taller with glasses. Here's the entry, the signature is illegible, the destination is Morecombe Industries."

"Morecombe Industries!" Harris repeated, "You've got to be kidding me! Arrest Kenny Everest, Basil Brush and Leonard Rossiter!"

"They're dead Sir, except Mr Brush, who's ... only a puppet," replied Jones, trailing off sheepishly.

Detective Harris said nothing, he didn't need to with that face. He glared at both men.

"What's next?  The Two Ronnies' Great Satirical Train Robbery?!!?"

"Sir?"

"Remember Ernie? Well this was Eric, this was both of them!"

"What?"

"It's a Morecombe and Wise Tribute Art Theft! Bring me some bloody sunshine!"

# The Salvaged Chair

The salvaged chair had been brought in from the workshop
Bare and raw, every last fleck of modesty scraped away
I saw it and blushed, deep and hot and prickly
My naked desire rocking back and forth in front of me
Exposing my whole world watching

# Which January?

January is a hungover sky, bruised and brooding and
   resentful,
January is a tightened belt around yuletide excess,
January is a lemon sorbet, clear and crisp and sharp,

January is an unmoored boat, trying out the flow,
January is the boring one, resentfully tidying after,
January is the first step of twelve, admitting we are powerless,

January is a dying firework, nearly out, making one last
   exhibition of itself,
January is a failed revolt, of resolutions by revolution,
   while patient evolution bides its time,
January is the first marks in the journal, determined this year
   will count.

# The Waterwheel

The brushed metallic surface absorbs the light,
dazzling flashes of azure and gold
no longer reflected,
the cold weight of the water is in the air,
the noisy warm softness of summer –
some long-gone stranger's memory.

# The Earth Turns

The earth turns towards the sun
edge of light rolling over mountains and seas
a wave of awakening
early with anticipation
or staggered late behind the dawn,

spinning slowly
warming then cooling
one seasonal pole missing out each turn
the other always in view
tilted towards our star
slipping back over the horizon at the equinox,

turning until darkness comes creeping over the horizon
darkness seeping over the rooftops
under doors, filling sleepy rooms
light dimming revealing further stars
and our one ivory satellite
while dancing fires of green aurora crown the ends of the earth,

across the diameter
on the opposite longitude
halfway around the circumference
imperfect symmetry of twelve hours forward
and twelve hours behind,

this marbled dot in the universe
this marvel of creation
our home.

# Breathing Underwater

Breathing underwater is easy when you are dreaming,
and gravity has no pull when I'm flying above it all,
I'm running through walls, into familiar buildings
that swap form and function, location and purpose,
distances contract and expand forever,
and those I recognise instinctively
live with different faces,

but awake, awake we can only fall, or drown,
this world of gravity and oxygen,
same faces in same places and rules,
rules against improbability,

so please write a story that's fantastic,
so I can return to my dream and
we can swim by the moonlight without drowning
and fly without falling,

a story of improbable happening,
of secrets of the heart and thoughts unfurled,
with new friends and new foes,

I'll read it overlooking the crashing foam,
from a mountain cliff,
until I'm ready to dive into the twinkling blue waters,
and surface somewhere new.

# Duality

Every place reverberates, resonates
Top notes and bass notes dance in rhythm and harmony
But in isolation, unconnected, each note may strike as both
  false and true
When I'm here I have my song, and when I'm there another
I am more of both each time I move and less of each as I stay
The sky is not the same sky, and the air is not the same air
  though it blows from there to here
And the sea is not the same sea though the water is cold and wet
The air is full of one or the other
Half of me is wanting away, half of me happy to be home
The comfort is that there is always the other half waiting for me
Out at sea I am neither, coming nor going
Close to land I'm leaving home and coming home with no con-
  tradiction
Stepping onto dry land I'm home to one but with only the deep
  memory of the other

For now when the present harmony runs out a deeper rhythm
  keeps me moving
until the new harmony is ready

One day I will feel different again
One day the music will change forever
I don't know how much of either tune will live on and what will
  fade away
But that song will come from deeper within, it's always been
  playing and one day I will hear it clearly.

# Autumn Drops

The sky has dropped,
now close enough to cast a line into,

The air has dropped too,
tired and thick, dragging its chill,

The carefree spontaneity of hot days,
disappeared into early hibernation,

Leaves are falling and turning,
moving through the colour spectrum,
green to red, or yellow, or brown
and every shade in between,

Petals scattered, the bare heads wait,
the last in the relay,
no fresh growth to bloom,

And fruit has dropped,
fractured in the fall,
to release their codes of life into the earth,
the last drunken wasp provokes, spoiling for a jab,

The tired sun, its radius shortened at the horizon,
  cannot climb above my eye,
an insistent bore, I avoid his gaze,

When it's over you have to, with regret, accept the changes,
What was warm and bright and full of promise,
(even when it faded there was a chance)
is now gone,

The point has passed, no sense hoping,
embrace, prepare, engage,
for now we work while we can, until the sun sets.

# Father's Day

We don't do Father's Day
Because we never did
And we never did because we never have done
It's our empty absent tradition
Our stand against coercion
Our sensible refusal of made up names
And he says nothing, it's his tradition too.

The church has donated a Sunday
So Mother's Day is on the calendar
Thanks for all you do for us, and did for us
Domestic drudgery acknowledged
Some flowers and an invitation to lunch
Which you will cook.

Father, Dad
No one sees what you do
at this place called work
For forty hours a week
Still no one's thanking you
We're keeping our tradition.

# Holiday with a Stranger

That first holiday with you
Meeting at the other end of the world
Cable car, crayfish, Kalk Bay
Catching the train up and down the coast
Taking photos of the penguins
And giant cacti in the botanical gardens
Seeing the prison, the quarry, and the isolating expanse of blue
The day with the silent hole in the middle, we never revisited
Me swimming in the ocean laughing off your concerns
Not knowing the patterns in motion
Sand dunes, ceramics, shortening our distance

A dozen years have passed
Opinions, preferences, priorities
Rolled out one after another
Reshaping every impression

Would I recognise you now as then
Did you know me then as now
Would I recognise you if we were blindfolded now,
  as we were then?

# Nursery Rhyme for Modern Times

Not the first and not the last
Pompous Pilot said, "I'll pass,"
he had the might but not the will
and let them take the Son to kill
washed his hands of one decision
just another politician

In the future just the same
wash your hands and pass the blame;

Minors mining, for cheap blood diamonds
pre-teens sewing jeans, poor and frightened

Appalli Nepali, hidden in the sands
world cup glory, for famous brands

Rowdy Saudis, buy another round
their enemy the Yemeni, don't hear a sound

Backing fracking, rupturing the land
unborn, too young, to take a stand

Smugglers charging a premium rate
while presidents ... just negotiate

We don't like the look of you visa-vis
turn a blind eye so we don't see

Life jackets floating by in the sea
You Don't Care So Neither Do We ...

# Surrendered Judgement

It's too late to care after all these years
washing your hands with crocodile tears

what was he to you, this King of the Jews?
an obvious pardon, but aggravation for you

release Barabbas roared the crowd
and history scored your cowardice loud

an act of indecision we still remember
a template for judgment to surrender:

clean air targets for all to meet
car-makers publicise all complete
but leave us breathless in the streets
exhausted by emission cheats

that coffee brand is grabbing water
with expired license, expensive lawyers
the common man must take a stand
as authorities look away, or sit, on their hands

\*\*\*

children meet your idols, secret games in the night
protection for our famous names, hiding in plain sight
dirty hands giving treats
wipe them clean on hospital sheets

favoured access, to young and new
the rich and famous, alone with you
stealing your youth with glamour and silence
our establishment condones the betrayal and violence

\*\*\*

carbon clouding up the air, cooking up creation
vote denial and leave it for, the next generation
and imprecise science is just an excuse
to carry on, with the abuse

dictators welcomed with open arms
diplomats impress that all are charmed
no-one mentions human rights
investment priority over innocents' plight

you are not the last and not the first
to find decision-making is cursed
a coward in the face of revolution
for a quiet life – an easy solution

how are your dreams, your conscience calling?
you saw the truth, and your star falling

you could have made the honest decision
not washed your hands, for your selfish vision

our hands maybe clean to the naked eye
but we will answer for this when we die.

# The Photographer's Assistant

## 1

Before we could all get back to our seats the announcement started. Mrs Huntley-Johnson, who I'd previously only seen from afar, or as a detail in her husband's photos, stepped up beside me. She looked proudly expectant. I was braced ready to offer my congratulations; although I still held a slight hope it would be me.

"And the winner of the best photographic portfolio of the year is ..."

The name wasn't mine. As applause broke out I smiled to cover my disappointment. Mrs Huntley-Johnson leant forward, as if to speak. I moved a little closer.

"Between you and me, I preferred yours," she whispered.

I turned, surprised by her indiscretion, to see her elegant profile staring straight ahead.

"You shouldn't really say that, should you?" I whispered back.

"I didn't really, no, it's very unlikely that I did," and with a wink she turned into the throng, weaving her way towards the stage where Mr Huntley-Johnson was shaking hands with the judging panel.

Those around me offered their commiserations.

"Better luck next time."

"Very good for a first effort, it must have been close."

"No one here expects to beat him, that's five years in a row now."

I wound my way back to my table.

"Sorry chaps, a bit of a melee at the tiramisu," I said in my most-posh voice.

"By jingo, I thought you'd gone and done it."

"Unlucky old chap – can I top you up?"

With the suspense finally broken I could at last relax, put the result behind me, and make a night of it.

## 2

Mrs Huntley-Johnson and I met again a fortnight later, quite by chance. As my train pulled in there she was, opposite me, reading a slim book, surrounded by empty seats. An expensive-looking silver scarf was draped around her shoulders, and an oversized handbag occupied the seat beside her. Looking up she caught my eye, so I said hello as you do, and sat down with the bag between us. We exchanged niceties and the conversation turned to the competition, and my pictures and how I'd taken them. I told her a little about setting-up and working and waiting; waiting for the best light, waiting for the right level of energy in your subject for the picture you want. From the conversation I soon realised she was clearly very knowledgeable about composition, if not photography itself.

"How much do you explain to the people posing in your photos?"

"Well, every project's different, but as a rule I'll tell them what I'm hoping for. It's teamwork, that's what makes a good model as well as a good picture. I'll have an end in mind, but sometimes I find new ideas as I go along."

She described spending hours sitting around in period costume while her husband adjusted lights and lenses and whatever else. I also got the impression she put her husband's prize-winning down to his choice of location, and little to do with talent. While I didn't doubt his technical ability, I hadn't found anything to love in his work, and not just because I'd lost to him.

"He's done a great job with the lighting, and you look good in the costumes," I suggested.

"Can you even see me? It could be anyone."

That was true.

"I'm quite bored of playing dressing-up. But he has to cast me in every shoot. Your way of taking photos seems much more ... useful."

I raised an eyebrow. She tried again.

"... Involved?"

"... Fun?"

"Fun, I'll take fun. Some interaction has to create a better picture. You could come and see how it works some time."

"Maybe I will," she said, followed by a hesitant, "would ... that be ... okay?"

"Sure, if you're free, and your husband hasn't already booked you, then yes, why not?"

She plucked her card out of her bag and handed it to me, "Do send a message when you're ready, just don't ask me to be a model, I've heard all about what happens. This is my stop so, cheerio."

I wasn't sure. Her saying "Maybe I will" was just polite, but the follow up had been uncertain, and sounded sincere. I'd thought over what she'd said the night of the competition. It was easy to dish out compliments and insincere flatteries in her position. I would have resented that had she not winked. The wink said that she meant it – that she preferred my work to her own husband's. And now she wanted to see how I did it.

## 3

A few weeks later, at dawn, Sasha Huntley-Johnson did join me. I'd planned to photograph where the countryside met the motorway, and was hoping for some moody shots of the sun rising contrasted against the early traffic. The light was worse than forecast and the photos weren't what I'd hoped for, and I wasn't in the best mood to be in the spotlight. I'd actually expected her to pull out or keep me waiting, but she hadn't. She'd been calm and inquisitive, and asked all the right questions, only once mentioning the damp cold and the early start.

As I dropped her at the end of her lane she did mention that she hadn't got around to telling Harold, her husband, about today and 'could I keep it under my hat' until she had. I said I understood, but I didn't see the big deal.

A week later I had a commission at a school in the next county, and I'd asked her along again. Just as well as these kids were a handful, and I'd never have got them organised for the group photos on my own. She was a natural, calling them out a class at a time, flattering them as they fussed over their appearance, leaving me to concentrate on the technicalities. The day went well and on the way back we laughed at some of the cheeky things the kids had said, like the one who'd asked if she fancied the headmaster (to which she had pointed to her wedding ring). But when I asked if she had any of her own the laughter ended. She turned away to stare out of the side window. I put the radio on to cover the awkward silence for the rest of the journey.

"I'm sorry," she said later as she gathered her things to get out of the car, "you caught me off-guard, that's all. I'm sorry if you think me rude, but I can't answer that question without ..."

"It's okay, it's your business."

"Maybe one day, once we've known each other longer. Thank you, I really have had a wonderful time. You will let me join you again?"

"Yes, of course, and sorry for ... I'll be in touch."

As she waved goodbye there were tears in her eyes. I felt guilty, but whatever I said would only make it worse. I watched her in the mirror as I drove away, wishing I could take back my words, and wondering what her story could be.

A few weeks later she did join me again, to photograph the early rowers on the river in Oxford. The mist hung low on the water, and condensation steamed off the crews like cigarette smoke, a perfect start to the day. Later we photographed the college buildings and grounds in the cool spring sunshine. She was easy company, nothing like the first impression she'd made. We talked of friends and places where we'd both been, and she amused me with stories of her husband's lecherous colleagues. Then I told her about my ideas for next year's competition.

"Good luck, for second place again," she said.

Not funny, and a little cruel. There was a long pause before she broke a smile.

"You'll win this year!"

"You think so? I'm up against some formidable competition."

"Yes, I do. Honestly, you should have seen your face!"

"Yeah, you got me."

Over lunch we talked of growing up. She told me about her younger sister and best friend Gwen. They'd started their schooling abroad, then boarding school in London together. Now she lives in Denmark with her husband and their three children, and they visit en masse every other year. But Harold has not been persuaded to take up the return invitation.

Neither of her parents were alive, her father passing away a couple of years after she was married, and her mother had died while Sasha was at university. It turns out that Harold Huntley-Johnson had been her first proper boyfriend. Her father had approved of the match and they'd married within a year of meeting. Soon after he died Gwen was posted to Brussels, and there was just herself and Harold, and that's how it's been ever since.

In turn I told her about my time as a journalist and photographer, amongst other jobs, and the places I'd been in Asia and the Americas, and some of the people I'd met and worked with. I told her about my younger brother and my best friend and stories of things we'd got up to as youngsters. We talked and talked and I told stories I'd not told for ages.

The afternoon turned into early evening and we walked back along the riverbank and found a pub. It was there that she told me about the social calendar which as "Mrs Huntley-Johnson" she's expected to attend, no matter how superficial. And the tedium of sitting around on Harold's photo-shoots came up again. She said she'd really like to do something for herself, to step out of the "role". Her husband wouldn't be happy so she hadn't raised it yet.

After that she wanted me to talk. I let on a little about my reasons for coming home, how I'd ended up where I was. She pushed a little on the details but let me divert the subject to music and art and books, or politics and religion and philosophy. I don't remember exactly which, but by the time it was dark we'd been through them all.

"Thank you, it's been a wonderful day," she said as she got in the car for the drive back. "I haven't talked like that for ages."

This time we drove home in a comfortable silence, with the radio on, all talked out.

## 4

My next project was a studio shoot, and I was hoping it would open some doors, and lead to some work with the photo-agencies. I'd hired four models and my idea was to concentrate on close-ups of body parts – a surface, a joint, a neglected angle. Sasha turned up early, arriving at the studio sensibly dressed in comfortable canvas shoes and light trousers, her auburn hair pulled back in a clip, and made herself useful.

We experimented with lights and postures, and the day quickly came together. Each model was photographed in close-up in the same position; and then all four together in one picture, close together casting parallel shadows on each other. We got the all the shots I wanted – the graceful corner of a bent elbow, the vulnerable exposed collarbone, the ankle joint in extension, the shoulders pushed back to their limit. The tricky bit was getting everyone in close and still and tense together for the group shots. Sasha was on hand to help each model, supporting the poses with cushions, or moving lights, and keeping everyone fed and watered. The pictures were turning out better than I'd imagined. In the afternoon we set up the second shoot – a rear quarter profile shot - taken from just out of sight behind the models. They just had to relax and resist looking back at the camera. Sasha stood a mirror on the far side for the models to focus on. It was starting to feel like teamwork, the first time since coming home.

The models were gone and as we were tidying up Sasha spoke up, "If I'd known the bare bits were going to be so respectable I might have volunteered a few bits myself."

"Really? Which bits in particular?"

"Oh, well …" she teased again, "I think I have quite nice feet."

"So let's take the shot. Let's take it now."

"I was joking!" she protested.

"I'm not – why not?"

"But you've got everything you need."

"We might get something better than we already have, you never know unless you try."

"But, I don't want to be in your project. I mean, I don't want anyone talking about me modelling, and all that."

"And all that? Okay, I do know what you mean. So, not your face, not your hands, something no-one will recognise, something no-one usually sees … like an elbow, or a knee."

"Oh I know your game, it starts with a knee, but where does it end?"

"At your toes, of course. Let's start with these nice feet you allegedly have and see for ourselves."

So she slipped off her espadrilles, rolled up her trousers, and I took a couple of shots of her slim, lightly freckled feet with their long toes and scarlet nails.

"Could I try something?" she asked.

I watched as she pulled out a thin silver necklace from under her shirt and wound it around one ankle. The next set of photos show a pair of lightly tanned feet, with one dressed with three turns of a soft silver chain at the ankle, resting on a damask cushion. It could have been anyone, but it could also only have been her.

"Is that me?" she asked.

"Just a bit of you, but yes definitely you."

"No-one would know from the photos would they?"

"Well, the chain might be a giveaway, but no-one would expect to see it there. And nice touch by the way."

She was clearly pleased and asked for another, so I took her rear quarter-profile shot. The photos showed her looking towards the background, away from the viewer, just the edges of her facial features showing, everything else hidden.

I emailed the best photos to her and deleted the originals as she'd made me promise.

"So, how was modelling?" I asked.

"Debauched, just like they say," she laughed. "I'm glad we did it, but you will keep it to yourself for now, until I get used to the idea."

"Of course, you have my word."

"Thank you."

5

A couple of uneventful weeks later, I'd just got off the phone when Sasha knocked on the open door of my office. Her eyes were flaming and her cheeks flushed. She pulled the door shut behind her.

"What's the matter?"

Sasha took a deep breath.

"Harold accused me of having an affair!"

"What? When?"

"This morning. He said he'd make sure everyone knew. He called me some awful names. I don't think I can go back there."

In all our time together there had never been any suggestion, not even a hint, that she was involved with anyone else. She had her complaints about Harold but there was never any suggestion of wishing for someone else. I didn't like the idea that this could be true.

"Oh Sasha, I'm sorry, really. What did you say?"

"I told him I'm not."

"Of course not."

"But I am aren't I? I am having an affair ... with you."

"But, we haven't even ..."

"Emotionally. Emotionally I am. You – you are where I want to be. I don't talk to anyone like I talk to you, and no-one listens like you do. You've made me question myself, who I thought I was, where I was heading. After each shoot I've just been waiting for the next one. Maybe that was wrong of me. But you've opened my eyes, shaken me up. Don't you see that?"

"I do – you've definitely changed – but I thought it was all you."

"No. No, it was you."

Sasha continued, "I've never done anything like this, never even been tempted. Harold accuses me of flirting sometimes, but I don't. I know I have a reputation for being aloof, and I'm glad of it. Even that first time with you wasn't really flirting. Except I winked, and I've never done that before. I thought it was nothing, but it wasn't. It wasn't just flirting, I really think I wanted you to rescue me. You made me wink, and now look what's happened. I can't ..."

She buried her head in my chest and sobbed, her breath coming full and heavy against me as I held her.

While we stood there holding each other I thought through the events of the past few months, revising each occasion in light of what had just been said. I'd been so unaware of what was really happening. I was proud and humbled at the same time. Yes she was attractive, but taken, and out of my league. After a while, when her breathing returned to normal, we pulled apart and she let me wipe away the mascara-stained tears that had trickled down her face, and I let her pick off a few stray hairs she'd left behind.

"How, are you?" she asked nervously.

"I'm okay, just thinking through what we've done, what I've been doing, how I thought I was keeping you at arms-length because you were married, ... are married."

"You did, and yes, I am. I'm still married. Yet I don't want to lose this and go back to how I was." She shook her head, "But I made promises, to forsake all others."

I caught a new tear before it reached the end of her nose.

"Now, I have something to tell you. Just before you arrived your husband called me. I'm meant to be taking his portrait for a book jacket this afternoon."

"What! Don't go! He must know – he must, why else would he ask you?"

"I don't know. He said he liked my work and wanted something different. Maybe he knows, maybe he doesn't, but I've got to face him sometime."

We sat and talked for a while. We were old enough to know we were still only at the beginning of a relationship, that we hardly knew each other. Maybe we had a future together. Much would depend on Harold's reaction – would he see it as her betrayal or his own failure?

There was so much we wanted to know from the other's perspective. But always there was the fact that she was still married. She would not break her promises, and I promised to stay away if I had to. This relationship was on hold until circumstances changed, however much we wanted to take the next step.

But all too quickly the time came for me to go. I promised to take care.

"Before you go, I have something for you," she said, plucking an envelope out of her bag.

Inside was a postcard-sized picture, the rear quarter profile picture. Taking a pen from my desk, she wrote in curling script on the back "This was the day you set me free."

6

Mr Huntley-Johnson ushered me in. So this was the place where she woke up every day, where she went after each time I'd seen her. Harold looked anxious, and I feared the worst. He led me to his study and sat himself behind a large desk. I set up quickly and took a selection of pictures. After I'd finished and he was satisfied with what he'd chosen, he sat back as if deep in thought. It didn't seem likely that I'd get out of there unscathed.

Mr Huntley-Johnson cleared his throat.

"I'd like to talk to you about my wife."

A cold sweat broke out across my neck.

"Um ... okay."

"I've done a terrible thing, to my wife."

"Sorry? – Why are you telling me?"

"Please listen, I have no-one else to tell." He leaned forward in his chair.

"Is this why you asked me here?"

"I've seen how you are with people. I know when people can be trusted. There's really no-one else, and you're not one of our circle."

He continued slowly, ignoring my protest, "My marriage is to my shame. I have treated Sasha terribly. It was at first a marriage of convenience. Even she doesn't know the extent of it. I need to tell someone."

"Oh then I have to stop you there," I interrupted. "Do you know I've been working with your wife? It wouldn't be right, to know what she doesn't. Our relationship may be professional, but she's become a friend. I don't want to know about her private affairs, especially if she doesn't know herself. You understand?"

"So you've seen the changes in her? She's become someone quite different. She's been in the garden all last week, digging and weeding and pruning and planting. I asked her why, when we have a gardener. 'It's more satisfying if you've done it yourself.' After her father's death I bought a piano, hoping it might help. But she played it once and never touched it again. Yesterday the housekeeper heard her playing. And she's talking of studying, and now you say she's been working with you – she never mentioned it. I found a sketch pad in the lower shed, two days ago, drawings of the dogs. They're really very good, but she hasn't shown them to me. She's making another life for herself. I think I married her too young. I won her over and put her on a pedestal before she'd had any experience of living."

Mr Huntley-Johnson paused, then continued slowly and carefully.

"And I denied her children. That was the cruellest thing I've done. That was the most shameful hurtful thing I could have done. It's no wonder she loves her sister's children so much. I should have ended this long ago, let her go, before it was too late."

There was nothing to say and Mr Huntley-Johnson was between me and the door.

"Sir, I really think she should be hearing this, and not me."

"You really do have a lot of respect for her don't you?"

"I do. She is intelligent, conscientious, and creative. And I'm beginning to respect her even more, for carrying this all along. Why did you wait until now?"

"I think seeing her change, seeing her happier than she's been for a long time, and knowing it's not because of me. She deserves to be free – she must want to be free."

"But she won't demand it, not at any cost to you. You've always known she would keep to the rules. That's why you chose her. That's why she's doing these things, working with me, sketching the dogs, so she has something of her own, outside of her life as your wife. Yes a secret life but still a faithful one."

"It's you isn't it? You! You're the reason for this change in her!"

I'd spoken too freely, giving myself away in her defence. Harold rose quickly to his feet.

"You've made a cuckold of me, and a fool of her, damn you!"

"No. No I haven't. Nothing's happened. She can't, and I won't. She only realised this when you accused her. And I was too blind to see it, too sure that she was out of reach."

Harold steadied himself.

"I really had never thought it would be you. That's why you said you didn't want to know, because she hasn't told you. Oh my dear boy, I do need a minute."

My mind raced back to that day at the school, when she'd shut down, when it had been too early to tell me why they were childless, and now maybe it was too late.

"You must hate me."

"I should, for her sake. But no, it's not hate."

"So, what are your intentions?"

"It depends – she is still married."

Harold seemed to have shrunk in stature and aged ten years since we had first entered this room.

"I could have set her free years ago, should have. It was selfish of me. It suited me and I didn't think I could cope. I didn't think I could keep it hidden, this … you know, I know how that sounds. And now she deserves better. I'll give her what she wants, you tell her that. On one condition. I mean, I have one request – please don't take her far away and disappear. I couldn't bear that."

Before I could respond there was a knock on the door, and Sasha entered silently. She beamed at me, and winked again, her fierce smudged eyes glistening with new tears.

"I couldn't stay away and so I couldn't help overhearing. Not all of it I'm sure, just from when you reminded my husband that I was still married. Thank you Harold for what you said." She turned slightly toward him, "I can't promise I won't go far, but I won't disappear."

Looking back up at me, the smile returned, her eyes crinkling.

"And you, you need to take me away from here, and show me how the other half lives."

So that's what I did.

And her eyes still crinkle when she smiles at me.

And when our children catch us winking at each other, they know we're keeping a secret, just between us.

# Into the Everlasting

This is not what I had expected when I turned the corner. I could hardly see anything. Grey forms, sad and ugly came into focus as my eyes adjusted. Where were the vibrant, colourful light-filled forms of previous visits? There was a heavy feeling in the air, of dread, of separation, of anger, and a sense of something worse coming. I felt trapped and alone, surrounded and lost. Had some force of darkness wiped through this place I had come to love? Where were the auras of light, or the pathway home?

I had followed the way here the same as every other time. I'd taken the usual precautions – it was too fantastic to risk losing the way. But here I was and all was grey, an ominous, silent scary darkness clung to everything, where before it had been bright and effervescence, a clear and melodious light in every direction. Shadows loomed close overhead threatening. The foreboding was spreading from my chest to my arms and I was physically shaking. I could see outlines moving in the distance but all the turning points were gone, the pillars of light that showed the way back. The entry point was there glowing and pulsating slowly in the murky gloom, an amber edge that showed where I had come in but could not return by. I tried to concentrate on the distance, beyond what I could see, hoping to summon a guideling.

I'd never had any difficulty before, in fact the first time the guideling had come naturally without asking, and maybe every time since. That first time I barely knew where I was, just that I'd left my material world behind, wondering lucidly whether I was dreaming or hallucinating. Before me was an immaterial world of light and shapes, shapes that could be called auras, a roundness larger than a human head with some kind of halo, lit by a light source that came from within, each with a crystalline structure at their centre. As I'd watched the auras shimmer and ripple, giving off a strong and strange sense of personality, a guideling had drifted up from beneath my feet. It was the most beautiful pulsating creature of light, which seemed to display every colour, every tone, every texture in a constantly evolving show, from metallic emerald to a soft flowery yellow, to blood red (via sparkly blues and velvet browns), to silvery white lace and shimmering black like the moon on the sea at night. I could have watched for hours, she was entrancing.

Then she spoke to me. I say she because the creature was so beautiful, and spoke in a careful comforting voice. And not that I heard it with my ears, but sensed it somewhere at the fore-front of my mind, a voice without command or malice, or suspicion or vagueness, a sense that all was well and going to be well, and going to be better too. And when she wasn't speaking there was a harmonious echo emanating from her.

So I did what I sensed she was telling me to do and I reached out to the nearest aura. At once, where there had been colour in blocks of the spectrum, these shimmered away until every colour, every kind of colour, appeared in an ever changing kaleidoscope. Within the aura the crystal formations were clear and reflected the light in twinkles or flat shines. Then she told me to reach out and I touched the colourless crystals.

Immediately I felt a pain. I first thought it was physical but I couldn't find the start or end point.

"This is their pain," said the guideling, "you must carry it back to your world for them."

"Why am I carrying their pain – and what will I do with it in my world?" I asked, distressed at the sensation of something for which I had no knowledge. It was a hard sorrow, like the memory of an undeserved rebuke from a friend.

"It will not go with you into your world, you just need to take it to the doorway. This is a pain you can carry."

"Should I go now? Where should I go?"

"You should touch the colourless crystals one more time."

I felt physically weighed down by the heaviness in my heart, and I was scared, so I looked for the smallest crystal in the structure. There was one next to a red cluster which glowing invitingly. Cautiously I tapped the small colourless one.

"You can only take the pain willingly. You will find the pain bearable, I promise."

I touched the crystal slowly. The distress hit me like a black wave, a memory of losing something valuable, of hopelessness towards it being recovered. But after it had hit me, it was bearable as she had said.

"You must return home now."

"How? What is this place? What are you? Will I see you again?"

"Don't be anxious, you will see us again. We are all part of the same. You will find us again like you did this time. You will only see one of us. We will guide you. You are one of those who will do great things for many people. Look into the centre, you will see the hard crystals are gone because you are carrying them, and the pattern is rearranged. The soul walks more lightly than before."

"Should I take more?"

"If you are overburdened you will not have the strength to make it home," her voice was soothing and familiar, like shallow waves rolling out on a stony beach, or wind stroking through high grass.

I looked around and saw vertical blue lights. There were many stretching into the distance but I sensed the nearest one was for me. I stepped towards it and around it. And with that I stepped back into the "real" world, the world I had always known and thought was real, but it seemed less real than where I had just been. It was a familiar place of pavements and faces, of noise and sunshine. A world that appeared much like the one I had stepped out of maybe hours, maybe moments ago. I felt giddy and flushed. The pain had gone. No sense of regret stayed with me. No memory except the certain memory of what had happened.

The place and the people were the same as when I'd taken that first step, that step towards and around the blue strip of light on the corner of the street, that had beckoned me towards it, and around the corner. Not this corner here which was just two walls meeting perpendicularly. I could see no blue strips here. I was only a short walk from where I had left, with its shoppers and buses and puddles in the street. Maybe it had been a dream, but it felt too real.

But if that first visit had been a vivid dream, this was a nightmare. The sort where you wake up and the terror stays with you. I did sense a guideling was close by, and I heard something but it was like voices underwater, and I couldn't see her in the dark gloom. Full of dread and scared to make a noise, I tried to will her to appear from wherever. A nagging fear was telling me there was no way out, there was nowhere to run.

In all my ventures into "the land of the everlasting" – as I had grandly named it in my head – this had never happened. I had reached out and taken the sorrow and pain and regret and endurance and perseverance, as much as I could bear. On occasions when I had overestimated my emotional strength the guideling had to warn me to take no more. Nearing full capacity, I had dragged myself to the nearest exit signal, and stepped away exhausted but relieved.

The guideling had always appeared to encourage me and thank me on the next visit. I had been gradually venturing further from the entry signal as I was led, and returning further away in the first world too. I called it the first world, but as it was unaware of the other, maybe it was really the second. Maybe before we are born we know this other world, and then when we are born our memories are cleared, so we are free from longing. I had asked a guideling where I was but she said it didn't have a name, only a purpose.

With reassurance from the guideling, I had started to take hold of the colour crystals. I found these carried more than one dimension of pain. As well as the carrier's pain or fear there was more coming from another source. The second distress hit me from a different direction like an undertow dragging at me, full of helplessness and fear at another's suffering, but it was okay, I could resist. I somehow knew this was shared pain and saw in glimpses that this new sorrow was from some other aura, a shared burden. Maybe somewhere else a glinting crystal was being released.

Over time, my strength had been increasing, and I had visited more than a dozen times by now. I was guided to touch more and more crystals, but only those that sparkled with light. Many just sat there reflective and dull, and touching them by mistake gave me a glimpse of their distress but there was no transference. I could now approach more than one aura on each visit, and I was beginning to understand what I was doing. The guidelings had said this would happen, although they wouldn't explain it themselves. I found I was also changing in my first world too. My patience and compassion was growing, I was becoming more aware of the needs around me, and I could feel my resilience and determination increasing to match, or I would have been overwhelmed.

I had many questions for the guidelings, but the answer was usually something they couldn't tell me, but declined so gently and sincerely that I was happy to accept, and not pursue. What I did now know was there were many others at work, although I did never see them.

So I would seek out a blue light, which was always on a corner, and head towards it and then turn into it. One time, early on, I turned into a corner and merely turned the corner, which was very upsetting. I thought I'd been excluded, I thought it had ended forever, that I had upset the guidelings and I'd never hear their harmonious, compassionate voice, or see their ever-evolving radiance again.

The blue light had gone out just as I turned, and I thought it was gone forever. I went home despondent. I thought back over what I might have done wrong. I wanted to see my guideling, she would have made sense of it for me. Later, I realised some-one had been close behind, close enough for my disappearing to be inexplicable.

The next day I went out early and there was a blue light on nearly every corner in sight. They had all come out for me. I was so relieved. But I was still worried it would happen again so I walked past the first corner. Immediately regretting my lack of faith I took the second, and I was back. The auras were waiting, the guideling floating up like a friendly jellyfish, then turning inside out into something like a metallic sea anemone, mottled and spiked, then softening again, lightening and expanding like a white chrysanthemum head, welcoming me home.

I had been starting to get a sense of the colours of the crystals, the circumstances of the experiences I was carrying back too. Fear, anger, desperation, anxiety, disappointment, betrayal, and how they connected to other people and health and loss and age and dreams. I wasn't getting all the details, I knew that would be too much to bear, but I was experiencing all the emotions, buried deep and echoing on.

But today the colours were gone. I had a growing fear that this was a darkness that wouldn't lift, an endless twilight of shadows of the unknown, angry and deceitful, bored and troubled.

The guideling was in front of me. I wasn't sure whether she had materialised or just come into focus but she was there white and delicate like a dandelion seed-head, softly rippling in an unfelt breeze. She didn't change pattern, just her colour and texture changing very slowly as if it was an effort, from white to silver to shiny black fibres and back again. My spirits lifted a little. Her voice was sorrowful and compassionate and missing the joyfulness she usually greeted me with. The dark auras (for that's what they were), moved as if agitated, heavy and scared, with thick spiked red crystals at their core.

"Do not fear. We are on the frontline. This is what your experience has been leading to. This is where souls are set free from their darkness. You will see flashes of red. Those are the cries we can take. You will be hit hard, by doubts, by regrets. You will want to run. See the green light that has opened ahead of you, that is the way out, that is the way home. Please listen. Everything I have said to you so far you have proven to be true. Remember this. Please. This is the most valuable work. What you did before was just a glimpse. You were harvesting fruit. Now you are mining for what is precious. I will be here but you may not see me, but I will be here, working with you. Please take a red crystal and hold onto it. Do not move until you know you can. Strength will come. Have peace my friend."

And with that she broke into tiny pieces, which turned in on themselves and faded in the gloom. It was like the softest light going out. Her echo grew feint until I could no longer hear it. She'd said she would still be here but I felt alone. Worse than alone. What I'd known was gone, and the loss was worse than being alone. Tears were in my eyes, and made the auras even more difficult to see. I stepped forward to the nearest one and reached out to glimmering red shards. As I took the glassy spike in my hand sorrow grabbed my heart with claws. As they sank in I felt a treasured love grow cold and hard, then fled from me at speed, tearing at my heart. Thoughts flooded my mind, not my thoughts but terrible thoughts of someone else. Despair and hatred, a seething anger and a loud sharp ache of unresolved doubt. Someone had gone and I hadn't been there to say goodbye, snatched away and now there were only bitter words and a gallery of words and faces that couldn't be trusted. Grief, like a belt around my chest and accusations like points of fire in my skull. Glimpses of a life of betrayal and judgement and worthlessness experienced that rang false. I tried to move but I felt I was being torn apart, skin splitting, my hip cracking and my ribs shearing. I remembered, or maybe she said it again, "hold fast". I held the pain. I endured the sorrow of the bereaved. I rode out the terror of violent acts. I took one step. I told myself, this is not me, it is going to be okay. I will hold fast. The pain increased, the belt tightened and the darts of fire pushed further in. The worthlessness felt deserved and I felt sick and weak. Help me. Hopelessness weighed me down. This is not true, this is not mine, love me. As the pain increased I felt my strength respond. As the belt tightened my chest pushed back. My hip cracked twice more like gunshots and the pressure broke. I forced a step towards the signal light. And another. An army of lies and insults and self-hatred assaulted me, punches that ran up my legs, and down my arms, but I knew they weren't mine. I waited, and in my head I repeated to myself, 'this is not true, love me'. As the pain increased again so did my determination and strength to match it. I held fast then stepped into the light.

I would do it all again for anyone of you.

# Reviews

Nick Horgan's crystal-clear and lyrical poems offer portraits of sadness and storytelling, struggles and joy. We get a sense of time passing and the poet's desire to extract meaning from small moments of everyday life. A pleasing, warm and very readable collection.
*David Gauntlett – Professor of Creativity and Design, and Director of Research, Westminster School of Media, Arts and Design, University of Westminster*

The writing is incisive, fluent and highly enjoyable to read. The poems explore a range of themes and ideas, including our relationship with nature, with the seasons and the events that we organise around them. It also explores the constraints of reality, versus the freedom of the human imagination.
   The poetry is full of vivid and interesting imagery; from the small moments in nature; beautifully captured; to a perspective of our earth within space, pulling us outwards. It is a contemplative collection that takes you through a range of experiences, from the collective gloom and resolve of January, to the playful rhyming on Guy Fawkes Night rituals.
*Rebecca Jones – Illustrator and Author of* Cat Disco

A Man and his World
   Like all good poets, Nick Horgan explores his place in the world and his relationship with it. In **The Earth Turns**, we sense the wonder of the whole planet, turning on its axis, as individuals respond – *a wave of wakening, early with anticipation, or staggering late behind the dawn.*
   **The Sun Came Out Today** explores the affect that a change in the weather can create, cleverly echoed by human relationships – *the sun didn't show today and neither did you.*

Horgan's work stretches from the metaphysical conversation with his god – **How Will You Answer My Prayer This Time?** – to the parochial – **Louder than the Wind**, which takes us from a sense of threat to the reassurance of human connection. In every case, the poet explores with fine imagery his place in the world and his relationship with his surroundings.

For me, the most powerful poem is **Asthma**. As someone who does not suffer from this debilitating affliction, I found that the imagery in this poem, ranging from straining trains to laughing tyrants to wooden lungs gave me an insight that I had never before had.

All in all, a fine set of poems that, through imagery and imagination, explore some universal themes from a very personal and distinctive perspective.

*Phil Lawder – Poet, Performer, Compere of the West House Open Mic Evenings in Pinner*

It may be self-evident to call Nick Horgan a poet, but not all who claim that mantle are truly worthy of it. Nick is, and that is his gift to the rest of us. In this collection we are at times faced with an honest and brutal critique of the world in which we find ourselves. Sweeping panoramic verses hover over the social, political and environmental issues that blight the planet. But lest we be quick to judge, Nick is not afraid to make the reader uncomfortable with the truth of our own complicity. Even when he turns to the familiar form of the nursery rhyme, there is no motherese, for he is all too familiar with the history of child verse to convey deep and dark undertones. And yet, buried among these ruins of modernity, Nick is able to point us towards a treasure, a hope which we are to give our all to obtain. Far from being beyond redemption, he paints for us a humanity who, in the words of John Steinbeck, is able to cry out, 'with all our horrors and our faults, somewhere in us there is a shining.' So it is, with tenderness and innocence, beauty and wonder, Nick lets us in to witness a more personal world. One

where nature isn't something to be exploited but cherished. A world in which the "Other" becomes a companion, empathy builds hope and home is where I choose it be.
*Alan Mann – Writer and Author*

Nick's poems have a world-weariness born of idealism and its consort, disappointment. This sense of discord is resolved only in the quieter moments, when the world meets what may be beyond. The powerful **Duality** is such a moment, beginning and ending as it does with the fundamental unity of all things. But eager that we don't ever become complacent, the poem's middle section returns to the differentiation and alienation so readily found wherever we are.

Responsibility and what it means are a golden thread shining through these poems. What are we to be held accountable for? **Father's Day** reminds us the biggest sins may be neglect and carelessness, while **Surrendered Judgement** offers cowardice and avoidance as the source of wickedness in this world. In other words, the poems show us that it is not what we do but what we do not do that is at the heart of the matter. It is a challenging message.

Meanwhile, "bruised" January just keeps on coming around, carrying echoes of Beckett. In this poem January doesn't exist as an independent fact but rather a projection of our burnt out expectations that things will ever change – or, as Nick so memorably puts it, "a dying firework, nearly dead, one last exhibition of itself." But there are intimations here that the fault may lie with our understanding of the world – our rules are fragile, our human systems pointless. This seemingly desolate message hints at a deeply mystical resolution, the opportunity for authentic change. You have to look hard but hope is secreted away in these poems, like the smallest, most precious present under the Christmas tree.
*Colin Bray – Service Development Manager, Libraries Unlimited*

Nick Horgan's poetry is both profound and accessible, so it's as captivating on the fifth read as it was at first. When I first read through this collection I relaxed into the phonetic beauty and potent imagery, and with each subsequent read I discovered a new depth of meaning behind and within each image. For example **Louder Than the Wind** plunges you into a musical moment sparking all five senses, before the perfect line "later I woke in a pile of friends ..." awakens the reader to the significance of a moment, that can only be realized with hindsight.

The collection is varied in style, content and tone, displaying Nick's creative versatility to evoke so much thought and feeling in just a handful of poems. Take **The Salvaged Chair** which, in only five lines playfully blends images of different types of desire, animating a seemingly mundane object. Whereas **The Earth Turns** uses its five stanzas to give a sense of awe at the majesty and magnitude of space, and a feeling of the oneness with humanity for the planet we share. The rich variety and depth of each piece gives a collection that is exciting, thought-provoking and appetising ... in that you'll want to read it over straight away!

*Peter Lilly – Poet and Missionary*

www.ingramcontent.com/pod-product-compliance
Lightning Source LLC
La Vergne TN
LVHW021545080426
835509LV00019B/2846